CLIFTON PARK-HALFMOON PUBLIC LIBRARY

W9-AHY-612

drug facts
STEROIDS

SUZANNE LEVERT with Jim Whiting

Clifton Park - Halfmoon Public Library
475 Moe Road
Clifton Park, New York 12065

Marshall Cavendish
Benchmark
New York

Marshall Cavendish Benchmark
99 White Plains Road
Tarrytown, NY 10591
www.marshallcavendish.us

Text copyright © 2010 by Marshall Cavendish Corporation

All rights reserved. No part of this book may be reproduced or utilized in any form or by any means electronic or mechanical, including photocopying, recording, or by any information storage and retrieval system, without permission from the copyright holders.

All websites were available and accurate when this book was sent to press.

Library of Congress Cataloging-in-Publication Data

LeVert, Suzanne.
    Steroids / by Suzanne LeVert with Jim Whiting.
        p. cm. — (Benchmark rockets : drug facts)
        Summary: "Discusses the history, effects, and dangers of steroids as well as addiction treatment options"—Provided by publisher.
        ISBN 978-0-7614-4352-0
1. Anabolic steroids—Juvenile literature. 2. Doping in sports—Juvenile literature. I. Whiting, Jim. II. Title.

RC1230.L482 2010
362.29—dc22
2008052752

Publisher: Michelle Bisson
Editorial Development and Book Design: Trillium Publishing, Inc.

Photo research by Trillium Publishing, Inc.

Cover photo: iStockphoto.com/Damir Spanic

The photographs and illustrations in this book are used by permission and through the courtesy of: *Shutterstock.com*: Istvan Csak, 1; Mathieu Viennet, 7; Cathleen Clapper, 14; Sascha Burkard, 15; Tootles, 17; Anyka, 23; Monkey Business Images, 26. *AP Photo*: Lionel Cironneau, 4; Damian Dovarganes, 16; Susan Walsh, 19. *iStockphoto.com*: angelhell, 8; Dennis Sabo, 22; Kris Hanke, 25. *SnapVillage*: Stephen Strathdee, 11.

3882

Printed in Malaysia
1 3 5 6 4 2

CONTENTS

A Growing Problem

IT WAS SEPTEMBER 30, 2000, THE LAST DAY OF competition at the Olympic Games in Sydney, Australia. The Olympic Stadium was packed with fans. One of the main attractions was American runner Marion Jones. Jones had already won gold medals in the 100- and 200-meter sprints. She was also the bronze medalist in the long jump and the 4 x 100 meter relay.

Many people believed these accomplishments were the greatest overall performance by a woman in Olympic history. Fanny Blankers-Koen of The Netherlands had won four gold medals in track and field at the 1948 London Olympics. But the level of competition in women's sports at that time was much lower than it was at the Sydney Olympics.

One thing was very clear. No woman had ever won five medals in track and field in a single Olympics. This was

Marion Jones (right) with her teammates at the Sydney Olympics.

Jones's chance to make history. She was running the third leg of the 4 x 400 meter relay.

The United States was in second place when Jones took the baton. She quickly rocketed into the lead and gave the team's anchor runner, Latasha Colander-Richardson, a 13.7-meter (15-yard) edge. Colander-Richardson lost a little ground to Lorraine Graham of Jamaica but still crossed the finish line in first place. Afterward, the relay team members posed happily for photographers, holding their gold medals in front of them. Jones's performance in Sydney brought her fame and riches.

But the smiles on that September day in 2000 would eventually turn to frowns. Rumors began to swirl that Jones had taken **steroids** in an effort to improve her running performance. Jones denied the rumors. She even testified under oath during a court case that she hadn't taken steroids. But the rumors never went away.

Finally, in October 2007, Jones admitted that she had taken steroids. Several months later, she began serving a prison sentence for lying under oath about her use of steroids. Her Olympic medals were taken away from her. From then on, Marion Jones would be known as a cheater.

Marion Jones is just one example of a growing problem in sports. This problem is the use of illegal steroids, and it's not limited to Olympic athletes. Many college and professional athletes take steroids. Steroid use even trickles down to high school sports. And athletes aren't the only ones who take steroids. Many young people take them in an effort to live up to unrealistic body images.

STEROIDS OCCUR NATURALLY IN THE HUMAN BODY. They are **hormones**, chemicals that carry messages to body tissues and vital organs and direct them to act in a certain way. Two of the most important hormones are **testosterone** (in males) and **estrogen** (in females).

Testosterone and estrogen control secondary sex characteristics. These include the growth of body hair, the deepening of the voice (in males), and an increase in breast size (in females).

Synthetic Steroids

Scientists can also produce steroids that are called **synthetic** steroids. There are two types of synthetic steroids—**catabolic** and **anabolic** steroids. In simple terms, the difference is that catabolic steroids tear down body tissues, while anabolic steroids build them up.

Catabolic steroids are used to reduce pain and swelling from muscle injuries or **chronic** joint problems such as arthritis, to treat allergies, and even to relieve the symptoms of chronic dry eye. Because of the possibility of severe **side effects**, doctors carefully regulate the use of these steroids.

Some people take steroids to help them build muscle mass.

The Muscle Machine

Problems with steroid abuse almost always involve anabolic steroids. Anabolic steroids affect the muscle system. The human body contains more than 650 individual muscles. In males, muscles account for about 40 percent of the total body weight. In females, the figure is about 23 percent.

The human body has three types of muscles. Heart muscles control the beating of the heart. Smooth muscles contract to enable us to digest food, urinate, and give birth. Skeletal muscles are the third and most abundant type of muscle. They are also known as voluntary muscles because we can control whether these muscles contract or expand. Most of the muscles work in pairs so that when one is contracting, the other is relaxing. For example, the biceps muscles allow us to flex our arms. The triceps muscles allow us to straighten them.

Skeletal muscles consist of many thin fibers, some over a foot long, yet thin as a human hair. These fibers are made up of **proteins**. The hormone testosterone sends signals to muscle cells to produce proteins to increase the size of muscle tissue. This is a natural process.

Skeletal Muscles

These illustrations show where some of the many skeletal muscles are found in the body.

The sternocleidomastoid helps move the neck from side to side.

The deltoids help move the shoulders.

The pectorals are the chest muscles.

The biceps bend the arms.

The rectus abdominus supports the muscles of the spine.

The quadriceps are the thigh muscles.

The trapezius covers the upper back.

The triceps straighten the arms.

The latissimi dorsi cover the lower back.

The gluteus maximus is the butt muscle.

The hamstrings are on the back of the thighs.

The gastrocnemius is the calf muscle.

An Unfair Advantage

Some people think that this natural process takes too long. They begin taking artificial steroids to speed up the development of muscle mass, endurance, and strength. Taking steroids becomes especially tempting for athletes, who believe that this will help them get college scholarships, professional contracts, and Olympic medals.

Taking steroids is cheating. It gives athletes who take them an unfair advantage over athletes who don't. Because of this unfair advantage, almost every athletic organization—from professional to collegiate to high school—bans steroids and penalizes those caught using them.

Taking Artificial Steroids

People who use artificial steroids swallow pills, inject themselves with needles, inhale nasal sprays, and/or apply creams or patches to their skin. Most users take steroids in cycles of 6 or 12 weeks. To increase the effects, users may "stack" or "pyramid" how they take the drugs.

With stacking, users take two or more steroids together. They believe that different steroids work together to produce a stronger effect than taking larger doses of a single steroid. Those who pyramid begin with low doses, gradually increasing them for a while, then tapering back down to zero use. Some users add a third period, in which they don't take steroids at all. They believe this steroid-free period allows the body's hormone system to recover. However, there is no scientific evidence that stacking or pyramiding produces the effects its users want.

Steroids and Body Systems

Taking artificial steroids is a risky business. That's because the effects of anabolic steroids aren't limited to muscle growth. These side effects extend to every cell in the human body and can affect several organs and body systems.

The Liver

The liver is the largest **gland** in the body. Its job is to rid the body of **toxins** and waste products. Because steroid doses are usually very high, the liver often strains to keep up with the amount of toxins it must get rid of. This can lead to cysts (small sacs of fluid) and even cancer.

The Kidneys

The kidneys also rid the body of waste products. Steroids can overwork the kidneys and lead to significant kidney damage.

The Cardiovascular System

The cardiovascular system consists of the heart and blood vessels. It carries oxygen and nutrients throughout the body. Steroids can damage this system in several ways.

- Steroid users often have high **cholesterol** levels. Cholesterol can block arteries and affect blood flow, leading to heart attacks and **strokes**.

- Tests on animals show that anabolic steroids can damage the heart muscle. The heart becomes weaker, making it less able to pump blood throughout the body.

- Steroids can increase water retention. This can lead to high blood pressure and a much higher chance of heart attacks or strokes.

The Immune System

The immune system consists of several glands that produce cells to fight infection and disease. Steroids can harm the immune system, increasing the possibility of becoming seriously ill.

Skin

Steroid use can cause high blood pressure. High blood pressure can cause the skin to turn red because blood vessels close to the skin pump the blood with more force. In some cases, the skin gets a yellowish tinge because the liver is working so hard. In a situation that is especially embarrassing to teenagers, most steroid users develop a skin condition called acne.

People with acne develop many large, red pimples on their skin.

Reproductive System

Steroids can make men unable to have children. Steroids can also cause men to lose some of their body hair. Their breasts can get larger and their testicles can shrink.

Artificial steroids are made from testosterone, which conflicts with a woman's natural estrogen. Many women on steroids have fewer menstrual periods, which may even stop altogether. It can be very difficult for women to become pregnant while taking steroids. Women may start losing the hair on their heads, their breasts may become smaller, they may begin growing facial hair, and their voices may become deeper.

Psychological Effects

Scientists who study the brain have found that steroids can disrupt the normal working of the brain and nervous system. This leads to several conditions.

- **Mood swings:** In the beginning, steroid users may experience good feelings. These feelings eventually change to sadness or anger. This is especially common in young teens. They are already having major mood swings as their bodies are flooded with hormones. Added steroids make the situation worse.

- **Increased aggression:** High levels of anger are common among steroid users. In one study, eight out of ten women said they felt more aggressive after taking steroids.

- **Reduced judgment:** The constant back and forth of mood swings may make it harder to make wise choices.

- **Depression and suicide:** Scientists believe that steroid use affects the production and use of **serotonin**, a chemical that regulates moods. When users stop taking steroids, they may become depressed and have thoughts of suicide. This situation is especially dangerous among people who are 15 to 34, the group most likely to take steroids.

- **Loss of sleep:** Many steroid users have a hard time either falling asleep or staying asleep. This is a big problem for teenagers who need lots of sleep.

- **Substance abuse:** Taking steroids may also lead to the taking of other drugs that are even more dangerous, such as heroin.

Skeletal System

Even before a baby is born, its bones are beginning to grow. This growth continues through childhood and into the teens. At a certain point, the concentration of testosterone signals the bones to stop growing. If this happens too early, the result is stunted growth. Then that person will end up shorter than he or she would have been without steroids.

In addition, steroids may change the size of the skull. In adults, steroid abuse can cause the skull bones to grow. In teenagers, it can stunt the growth of the skull bones. In some cases, it is possible to tell if a person is on steroids simply by looking at the shape of his or her face and skull.

Other Dangers

In many cases, steroid users have no idea if the steroids were made under safe conditions. Often steroids are combined with other drugs. Sometimes people even take steroids that are meant for animals. This means users can ingest harmful chemicals. Because some users inject steroids and then share the needles, there's also a chance they can become infected with deadly diseases such as HIV.

As is the case with other drugs, there is always the risk of becoming **addicted** to steroids. The drug becomes the main focus of the user's life, and the user may even turn to crime in an effort to get money to buy the drugs.

People don't only take steroids to improve athletic performance. They may also take steroids in a mistaken attempt at improving their body image. Take Stacy, for example. She was 13 when she started to worry about her body image and 15 when she started taking steroids. It took her four years to kick her steroid habit. Stacy now looks back on her high school years with sadness and regret.

"I hated the way I looked in high school. Hated it. I felt pudgy and dumpy, even though I was at a normal weight for my body type. No matter how much I worked out, I never looked like the models I saw on TV, or even the cheerleaders at my school. My friend's brother, a college football player, started me on steroids. I took oral steroids—I never used needles. It worked for awhile. I did change the shape of my body. But the price was too high. My breasts practically disappeared, I had awful mood swings and, worst of all, I had to hide a huge part of my life from my family and friends. I didn't have to worry about getting caught—my friend gave me the steroids and my school didn't have **random** drug-testing— but I felt awful about it, all the time. I felt like I was a fake."

Steroids and the Law

IN 1988, THE U.S. CONGRESS PASSED THE ANTI-DRUG Abuse Act. It became a crime to use or sell anabolic steroids for non-medical purposes. Two years later, the Anabolic Steroid Act put the U.S. Drug Enforcement Administration (DEA) in charge of enforcing the laws against steroids.

People who are caught using or selling steroids can go to prison.

The law treats offenses seriously. For a first offense, a person may go to federal prison for up to five years and pay a fine of up to $250,000. For those convicted a second time, the penalties double—up to ten years in jail and a $500,000 fine.

People continue to use steroids in spite of the law and its penalties. Where there's a demand, there will always be a supply. According to estimates, the illegal trade in steroids amounts to several billion dollars every year. Secret laboratories in the United States and around the world produce the drugs. Drug dealers sell them directly to consumers.

Being caught with drugs isn't the only legal risk that steroid users take. Steroid users break the law if they lie in court about their involvement with steroids. This can lead to a prison sentence, such as the one given to Marion Jones.

So how do authorities determine if a person is using steroids? They use drug testing. Traces of artificial steroids may remain in the body for up to a year and can be detected through special tests.

Testing began in the 1950s when Italian athletic officials wanted to see if soccer players and bicycle racers were using drugs. Athletes at the Olympics were tested for the first time in 1976. While athletes are the main focus of drug testing, more and more people at school and in the workplace are being tested, too.

This technician is testing urine samples for steroids.

The easiest method of testing is with a urine sample. In some cases, the top finishers in a sporting event must immediately provide a sample. In other cases, the tests are carried out at **random** without prior warning. Those chosen for testing also give a urine sample. Trained **technicians** test the urine for steroids. Blood can also be used for testing. It's a more accurate test, but it's also more expensive and complicated. Drug testing stops many athletes from taking steroids because they don't want to risk their reputations and careers. However at least one-third of all young people taking steroids are not athletes, so drug testing doesn't encourage them to stop.

Many young people feel they don't need a test to tell them who is taking steroids. Thirteen-year-old Samantha says, "It's pretty easy to tell when people are using steroids, even without a test. People get moody and their skin breaks out, and they never seem to get tired."

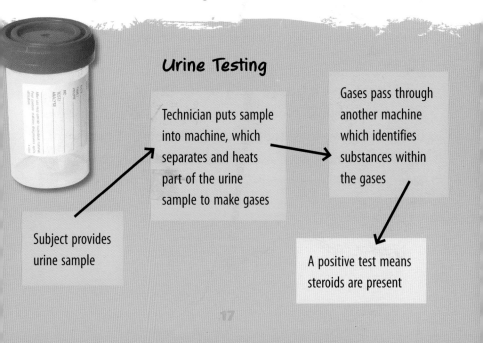

Urine Testing

Subject provides urine sample

Technician puts sample into machine, which separates and heats part of the urine sample to make gases

Gases pass through another machine which identifies substances within the gases

A positive test means steroids are present

Drugs and the U.S. Constitution

Some people object to the whole idea of testing, whether for steroids or other drugs. They say that the Fourth Amendment to the U.S. Constitution protects citizens from unreasonable searches. For example, police need **probable cause** before going into a person's house to look for evidence. They have to convince a judge to allow them to search. In the case of drug testing, some people say that obtaining random urine samples is an invasion of privacy.

In several recent cases, the U.S. Supreme Court has said that random drug testing is **constitutional**. One case involved railroad workers. The Court decided that passengers could be in danger if railroad employees were using drugs. The Court felt that passenger safety was more important than the employees' right to privacy.

Another case involved workers who handled guns as part of their job. In this case, the Court also ruled that public safety was more important than the employees' right to privacy.

A third case related directly to the use of drugs in high school and college sports. The Court decided that random drug testing was constitutional under the Fourth Amendment. The Court said safety issues made the testing reasonable. Safety issues were more important than privacy rights. The Court added that random testing didn't discriminate against anyone.

Graham Boyd (center) was an attorney for the American Civil Liberties Union representing Tecumseh School District students' challenge of random drug testing at their school. The U.S. Supreme Court ruled that the random drug testing could continue.

Should Steroids Be Legalized?

Some people say that drugs like steroids should be legalized. They argue that it costs a lot of money to investigate and catch people accused of buying and selling drugs. They point out that it also costs money to keep prisoners in jail. People also argue that there would be more control over the manufacture and sale of steroids if they were legal. They believe the drugs would be safer.

The Role of the DEA

The U.S. Drug Enforcement Administration (DEA) was created in 1973 by President Richard M. Nixon. Today the organization has more than 5,000 agents and offices in more than 60 countries around the world. Many of these agents concentrate on tracking down buyers and sellers of steroids.

The DEA has caught many buyers and sellers. Perhaps the most spectacular success came in 2007 during Operation Raw Deal. Following a two-year investigation that involved working with several other agencies, DEA agents arrested nearly 150 people and seized 11.4 million steroid dosage units.

A third argument for legalizing steroids is that users would then be under the care of doctors. With doctors in charge of the amount of steroids a person takes, the side effects could be reduced.

Those against legalizing steroids say that most, if not all, of the health risks would be the same whether steroids are legal or illegal. They believe legalizing steroids would encourage people to try to change their bodies, at a risk to their health. They add that taking steroids would still give an unfair competitive advantage to athletes who take steroids over those who don't.

Steroids Timeline

1935   German scientists develop artificial steroids.

1950s   Italian government begins testing soccer players and cyclists.

1973   DEA created by President Richard Nixon.

1975   International Olympic Committee bans use of steroids.

1976   Olympic Games in Montreal are the first Olympic Games where drug testing is used.

1988   Canadian sprinter Ben Johnson sets world record in 100-meter dash in the Olympics but is later disqualified for using steroids.

1988   Anti-Drug Abuse Act passed by U.S. Congress.

1990   National Football League begins program of year-round steroid testing, choosing players at random.

1996   Baseball player Ken Caminiti wins the National League Most Valuable Player Award; later admits he used steroids; dies of heart attack at age 41 in 2004.

1999   International Olympic Committee establishes World Anti-Doping Agency.

2004   In his State of the Union Address, President George W. Bush urges professional sports to get rid of steroids.

2006   American cyclist Floyd Landis wins the Tour de France bicycle race but loses title when tests reveal traces of steroids in his system.

2007   Baseball player Barry Bonds breaks Henry "Hank" Aaron's career record for home runs; many believe he used steroids.

2007   Operation Raw Deal arrests nearly 150 people and seizes 11.4 million dosage units of steroids.

2008   Marion Jones sentenced to six months in prison for lying about steroid use.

4 Quitting Steroids

IT SEEMS LIKE TREATING PEOPLE WHO ARE TAKING steroids would be very simple. After all, they just need to stop, right? Unfortunately, it's not that easy for people to stop once they are used to taking steroids.

Many young men and women take steroids to improve their low self-image. For these people, steroid abuse is often related to eating disorders. While it is mostly women who suffer from eating disorders, some men do, too. New evidence suggests that some men may also have another condition that puts them at risk for using steroids. This condition makes them obsess about lacking muscle definition, even if they do have muscular bodies. In order to stop taking steroids, these young men and women first need to deal with their low body image.

Regular exercise is a healthy way to build muscle and keep fit.

People experience **withdrawal symptoms** when they try to stop taking a drug to which they are addicted. This makes it very hard and very painful for them to stop. Withdrawal symptoms can include the following:

- Depression
- Headaches
- Sleeping difficulties
- Nausea
- Excessive sweating
- Weight loss
- Muscle shrinkage
- Loss of energy
- Extreme fatigue
- Restlessness
- Craving for steroids

Researchers don't completely agree about whether or not steroids are addictive in the same way that heroin, cocaine, or other deadly drugs are. However, more and more studies show that steroid users do suffer from withdrawal symptoms similar to users who stop taking drugs like heroin or cocaine. A study in Britain in 1991 found that the most frequently reported withdrawal symptoms for steroids users were: cravings for steroids (52%), fatigue (43%), depressed mood (41%), restlessness (29%), headaches (20%), falling asleep (20%), and decreased interest in sex (20%). These symptoms happen because the body and mind of the user have become dependent upon the effects of the steroids in order to feel "normal."

Sixteen-year-old Jason had first-hand experience with many of these symptoms. He had begun taking steroids to improve his performance on his school's wrestling team. He stopped taking them when the coach announced that the team members would be tested for steroids. It didn't take long for him to feel the effects.

"I felt depressed and edgy at the same time," Jason recalled. "I had headaches, too. I didn't give in, but I did keep thinking that if I just took a little more of the steroids, then I'd feel better."

Jason was lucky to be able to quit. Eventually the headaches and the other symptoms went away. The experience was a valuable lesson for Jason. He vowed never to use steroids again.

Jason was able to quit taking steroids on his own. Other users may not be able to do it by themselves and may require help. A doctor or psychologist can offer support to help the user deal with the side effects of withdrawal. Other sources of support include teachers, school counselors, and coaches. Local mental health agencies and drug abuse centers can also provide help and encouragement.

In more severe cases, users may have to go to a hospital for treatment or go on medication. Some medications help restore the hormone system. Other medications may target specific symptoms. For example, former users who become severely depressed may be given medications that help them deal with their depression.

People use their own body weight as resistance when they do exercises like push-ups.

People take steroids to become better athletes or to try to improve their body images. If they stop taking steroids, how do they deal with their original reasons for taking the drug?

The best way is through a good diet and regular exercise. Building muscle requires adding resistance to normal body movements. This resistance makes muscles contract with increased tension. The increased tension causes them to grow larger and become stronger.

There are two ways of doing resistance exercise—through exercises like push-ups, which build muscles by using a person's own body weight as the resistance, and by lifting weights or using weight machines. Training with weights builds muscle more quickly because weights provide more resistance and make muscles work harder. However, teens need to work with a professional instructor to avoid injury from lifting weights that are too heavy.

Whatever type of exercise people do, it's best that they seek the advice of qualified professionals to avoid injury. This is especially important for young people. A study in 1998 showed that of the estimated 60,000 injuries linked to weight-lifting equipment, 35 percent involved people age 15 to 24, and 12 percent were linked to children age 5 to 14.

Stacy remembers quitting steroids during her first year in college.

"At first, it was really hard. I had to work harder to keep my shape. But then I started playing tennis—I'd never been athletic at all—even though I used steroids!—and found that although I would never be mistaken for a model, I felt so much better about myself, stronger even, prettier even. My female shape began to come back, and I felt better physically. It sounds like a cliché but regular exercise and a good diet do more for you all around than any drug."

A Plan for Staying Healthy

- Work with a coach or fitness trainer to help set goals and learn proper techniques.

- Aim for exercise that is challenging. "No pain, no gain" is a myth. People need to feel challenged by their routine but should never feel pain.

- Choose enjoyable activities to keep exercise interesting and to avoid boredom or dissatisfaction.

- Make a commitment to hang in there and stick to a set schedule.

- Be aware that safety comes first in order to avoid injury.

- Eat healthy foods.

In addition to exercising to build muscle, a balanced diet is important to provide the body with the nutrition it needs. Muscle tissue needs protein to grow, so proteins should make up at least 10 to 15 percent of a daily diet. **Carbohydrates**, particularly those in whole grain breads and pasta, are necessary to provide energy. Fruits and vegetables contain vital vitamins and minerals.

Weight training by itself may not be enough to achieve a fitness goal. Other activities such as running, bicycling, swimming, and hiking make a well-rounded program. Young people can also consider trying out for sports teams at their high school. That way they get the benefit of learning proper techniques along with working with others toward a common goal.

GLOSSARY

addicted: Having an ongoing physical demand for a harmful substance.

anabolic: Promoting the growth of tissue; from a Greek word that means "to build up."

carbohydrates: Types of food that provide the body's main source of energy; primarily sugars and starches.

catabolic: Breaking complex substances down into simple ones; from a Greek word that means "to throw down."

cholesterol: Fatlike substance found in the liver, brain, bile, etc., that is essential to many body functions; too much can contribute to heart disease.

chronic: Constant; continuing over a long period of time.

constitutional: Permitted by government laws.

estrogen: Female hormone responsible for development of secondary sex characteristics; largely produced in the ovaries.

gland: Organ that produces a fluid for use in the body.

hormones: Chemicals produced by glands that have specific effects on organs and body processes such as growth, sexual development, metabolism, and sleep patterns.

probable cause: Reasonable suspicion that a person has committed a crime and should be investigated.

proteins: nutrients that are an important part of all living cells and necessary for life.

random: Without any fixed order.

serotonin: Chemical that occurs naturally in the body and is associated with good moods.

side effects: Additional results from taking a drug, usually not desirable.

steroids: Hormones that regulate and control numerous body functions.

strokes: Sudden losses of consciousness or the ability to move as the result of a rupture of blood vessels in the brain.

synthetic: Produced in a lab by humans.

technicians: People who are trained and skilled at a particular job, such as testing for drugs in a lab.

testosterone: Male hormone responsible for development of secondary sex characteristics.

toxins: Harmful substances; poisons.

withdrawal symptoms: Uncomfortable, stressful physical and psychological effects or changes that happen after abruptly stopping a drug or addictive substance.

FIND OUT MORE

Books

Hatton, Caroline. *The Night Olympic Team: Fighting to Keep Drugs Out of the Games*. Honesdale, PA: Boyds Mills Press, 2008.

Lau, Doretta. *Steroids (Incredibly Disgusting Drugs)*. New York: Rosen Central, 2008.

LeVert, Suzanne. *The Facts about Steroids*. New York: Marshall Cavendish, 2005.

Naden, Corinne. *The Facts about the A–Z of Drugs*. New York: Marshall Cavendish, 2008.

Schaefer, Adam Richard. *Steroids (Health at Risk)*. Ann Arbor, MI: Cherry Lake Publishing, 2008.

Walker, Ida. *Steroids: Pumped Up and Dangerous*. Broomall, PA: Mason Crest, 2007.

West, Krista. *Steroids and Other Performance-Enhancing Drugs*. New York: Chelsea House, 2008.

Websites

National Institute on Drug Abuse
http://www.nida.nih.gov/Infofacts/Steroids.html

Nemours Foundation
http://www.kidshealth.org/teen/drug_alcohol/drugs/steroids.html

Partnership for a Drug-Free America
http://www.drugfree.org/Portal/Steroids/index.html

U.S. Department of Health and Human Services and SAMHSA's National Clearinghouse
http://ncadi.samhsa.gov/govpubs/phd726

INDEX

Page numbers for photographs and illustrations are in **boldface**.

OCT   2010

CLIFTON PARK-HALFMOON PUBLIC LIBRARY, NY

0 00 06 0365388 2